IRELAND

IRELAND

Photography

TIM THOMPSON

Essay

SUSAN POOLE

GRAPHIC ARTS CENTER PUBLISHING COMPANY, PORTLAND, OREGON

International Standard Book Number 1-55868-125-6
Library of Congress Number 93-70109
© MCMXCIII by Graphic Arts Center Publishing Company
P.O. Box 10306 • Portland, Oregon 97210
No part of this book may be reproduced by any means
without the permission of the publisher.
President • Charles M. Hopkins
Editor-in-Chief • Douglas A. Pfeiffer
Managing Editor • Jean Andrews
Designer • Robert Reynolds
Production Mgr. • Richard L. Owsiany
Cartographer • Ortelius Design
Typographer • Harrison Typesetting, Inc.
Color Separations • Agency Litho
Printer • Dynagraphics, Inc.
Bindery • Lincoln & Allen
Printed in the United States of America

To my wife Eva, who patiently watched me wander
off repeatedly into the Irish landscape, and
for my two boys, Brandon and Darrin, who had a
summer to learn of a part of their heritage.

TIM THOMPSON

◄ ◄ A mystical air hangs about the Cliffs of Moher, which
rise to some seven hundred feet. Nearly five miles long and
one of County Clare's most outstanding features, the cliffs
afford breathtaking panoramic views of the Atlantic coast,
with the offshore Aran Islands plainly visible on a clear day.
O'Brien's Tower, built early in the nineteenth century, crowns
the northern end where they are highest, while Hag's Head at
the southern end reaches only some four hundred feet high.

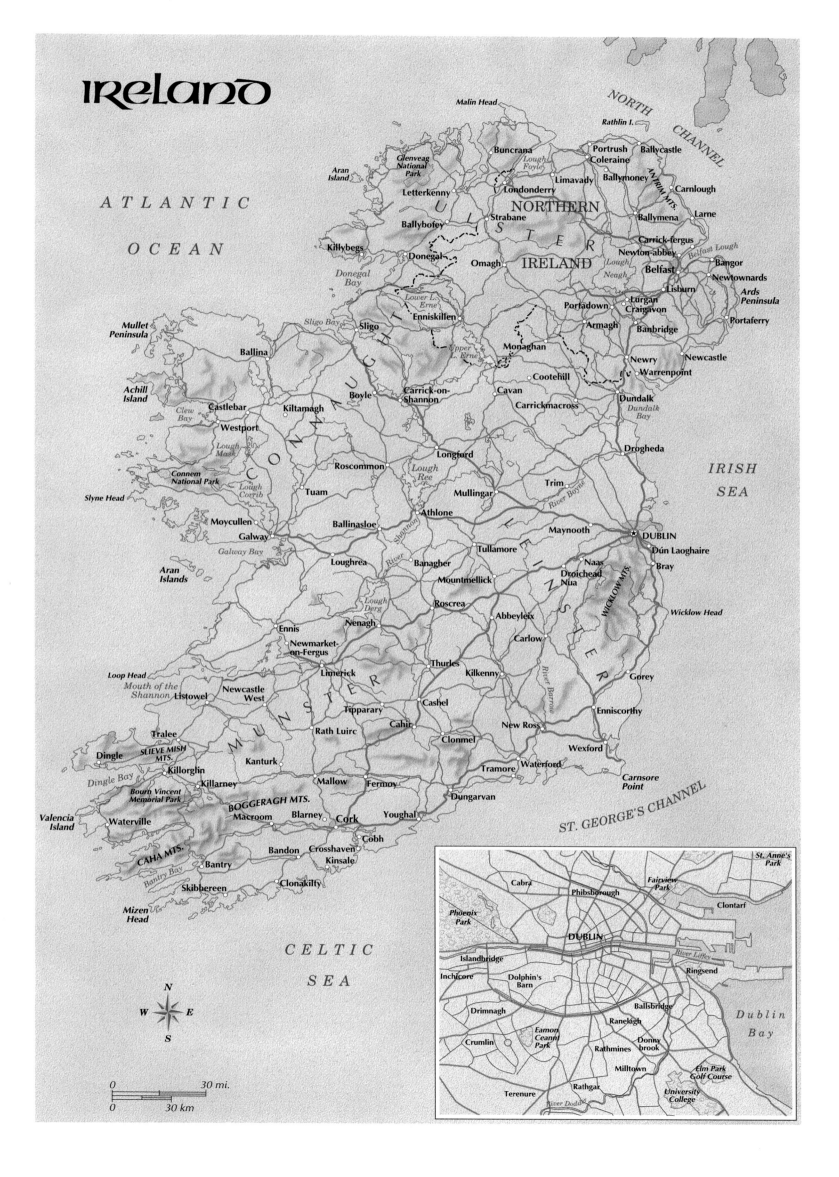

Ireland

ATLANTIC OCEAN

NORTH CHANNEL

Malin Head

Rathlin I.

Aran Island

Glenveag National Park

Buncrana

Portrush
Coleraine
Ballycastle

Lough Foyle

Limavady
Ballymoney

Carnlough

ANTRIM MTS.

Letterkenny

Londonderry

NORTHERN

Larne

Ballybofey

Strabane

ULSTER

Ballymena

Carrick-fergus

Killybegs

Omagh

IRELAND

Newton-abbey

Bangor

Donegal

Lough Neagh

Belfast

Newtownards

Donegal Bay

Lurgan
Craigavon

Lisburn

Ards Peninsula

Lower L. Erne

Portadown

Mullet Peninsula

Sligo Bay

Enniskillen

Armagh

Banbridge

Portaferry

Sligo

Upper L. Erne

Monaghan

Newry
Warrenpoint

Newcastle

Ballina

Cootehill

Dundalk

Achill Island

Boyle

Carrick-on-Shannon

Cavan

Carrickmacross

Dundalk Bay

Clew Bay

Castlebar

Kiltamagh

CONNAUGHT

Westport

Lough Mask

Longford

Drogheda

IRISH SEA

Connem National Park

Lough Corrib

Roscommon

Lough Ree

Trim

River Boyne

Slyne Head

Tuam

Mullingar

Moycullen

Ballinasloe

Athlone

Maynooth

DUBLIN

Galway

Tullamore

LEINSTER

Dún Laoghaire

Galway Bay

Loughrea

Banagher

Naas
Droichead Nua

Bray

Aran Islands

Mountmellick

WICKLOW MTS.

Wicklow Head

Lough Derg

Roscrea

Abbeyleix

Ennis

Nenagh

Carlow

Newmarket-on-Fergus

Thurles

Kilkenny

River Barrow

Gorey

Loop Head

Limerick

MUNSTER

Cashel

New Ross

Enniscorthy

Mouth of the Shannon

Listowel

Newcastle West

Tipparary

Rath Luirc

Cahir

Clonmel

Wexford

Tralee

SLIEVE MISH MTS.

Kanturk

Tramore

Waterford

Carnsore Point

Dingle

Killorglin

Mallow

Fermoy

Dungarvan

Dingle Bay

Killarney

BOGGERAGH MTS.

Youghal

ST. GEORGE'S CHANNEL

Bourn Vincent Memorial Park

Macroom

Blarney

Cork

Valencia Island

Waterville

Cobh

CAHA MTS.

Bandon

Crosshaven

Bantry

Kinsale

Bantry Bay

Skibbereen

Clonakilty

Mizen Head

CELTIC SEA

N
W E
S

0   30 mi.

0   30 km

St. Anne's Park

Cabra

Phibsborough

Fairview Park

Clontarf

Phoenix Park

DUBLIN

Islandbridge

River Liffey

Ringsend

Inchicore

Dolphin's Barn

Dublin Bay

Drimnagh

Ballsbridge

Eamon Ceannt Park

Ranelagh

Donnybrook

Elm Park Golf Course

Crumlin

Rathmines

Milltown

University College

Terenure

Rathgar

River Dodd

◄ Sheep farming is one of the island's most important agricultural industries, with pastures often extending to the cliffs, as here, above the Giant's Causeway in County Antrim.
▲ Dunluce Castle, in Northern Ireland's County Antrim, sits so close to the cliff that in 1639 part of it fell into the sea.
► ► Crashing waves carve striking formations out of the cliffs of County Mayo's Achill Island, creating a pure meeting of land, sea, and air – the three essential elements of earth.

▲ The ancient crafts thrive in modern Ireland. An order of
Benedictine nuns rely on their prosperous pottery industry
to help sustain the Kylemore Abbey, a nineteenth-century
castellated stone mansion. Built as a private residence,
and now an exclusive girls' school, the abbey nestles on the
wooded banks of Pollacappal Lough in the Pass of Kylemore.

▲ Seafood lovers, who have long dismissed Irish cuisine as strictly "meat and potatoes" and bemoaned the lack of imaginative dishes incorporating denizens of Irish waters, are in for a surprise. Bounteous harvests from the sea, river, and lakes, as typified by this Dingle display, yield Dublin Bay prawns, lobsters, and Galway Bay oysters, as well as the famed Irish salmon, sea trout, brown trout, and sole, all of which come to table in creative as well as traditional dishes.

▲ In County Westmeath, these fresh-faced colleens in the ecclesiastical town of Mullingar, whose skyline is dominated by the lofty Cathedral of Christ the King, show off their lovely First Communion dresses. So important is this occasion that Irish mothers spare neither effort nor expense in choosing their offsprings' attire for the event, even though the dress, like a wedding dress, will be worn only once.

▲ *Cashel* in Irish means "stone fort," and the Rock of Cashel, which served as the magnificent citadel of Munster kings from A.D. 370 to 1101, resisted attacks for centuries. From the vantage point of its three-hundred-foot perch above the Tipperary plains, even its ruins appear as impregnable today as when St. Patrick dropped by in A.D. 450, to be followed by later visitors such as King Henry II and Edward the Bruce.

▲ A West Cork fishing village, Baltimore has drawn both friend and foe from the sea. The village suffered a tragedy of epic proportions in 1631, when raiding Algerian pirates killed many inhabitants and shipped others to North Africa as slaves. Today, proud boat owners keep their paintbrushes busy, sometimes cleaning them against the dockside rocks.

▲ The mystical side of Ireland is reflected in the other-worldly vastness of the Burren in County Clare, whose strange, lunar-like limestone surface nurtures myths and legends galore, as well as the most remarkable collection of flora species in Ireland. Many are found nowhere else in the world. Beneath the Burren's scarred surface lurk spectacular caves, streams, and turloughs – lakes that disappear in summer, only to magically refill when winter arrives.

▲ In times past, life was perilous in Clonmacnois, County Offaly's holiest of holies. Not even the presence of kings and ecclesiastics could keep the settlement safe from raids by native chiefs, the Danes, Anglo-Normans, and Cromwell on his devastating sweep through Ireland in the seventeenth century. Its holy, but unhappy, past is mirrored in a cathedral, eight church ruins, two round towers, three sculptured high crosses and the remains of two others, and a ruined castle.

Ireland

by Susan Poole

A LOVE AFFAIR. "Sure, a little bit of heaven dropped from out the sky one day." So goes the old song about Ireland, and when I first set foot in the country back in the early 1970s, my instant reaction was a hearty "Amen." I stayed three weeks that year, and yearly visits thereafter finally led to a move across the Atlantic to make Ireland my home. Those years have put very human feet under that heavenly vision, but my love affair with Ireland has dimmed not one whit, only grown stronger with each passing year.

Although more than one friend accuses me of being besotted with Ireland, I have come to know that my affection is by no means unique – the very mention of Ireland to anyone who has ever been here elicits accolades like "magical" and "mystical." In truth, there *is* something magical about Ireland. The ingredients of that magic are a potent blend of incomparable scenic beauty, an incredibly long and convoluted history, and a people who color the very air with their remarkable way with words – words vibrant with wit, compassion, and basic human values that have survived intact through centuries of turmoil. Small wonder, indeed, that Ireland casts its spell on all comers.

As one who is firmly enmeshed in that spell – and especially as a writer – I am intrigued by the myriad of detail, human and physical, involved in the complexity that is Ireland. As other writers have discovered, the challenge of capturing its uniqueness in mere words is a never-ending torment. "I am beginning to find out now that a man ought to be forty years in this country instead of three months, and *then* he wouldn't be able to write about it!" is the way William Makepeace Thackery expressed it back in 1842. All one can hope to do is evoke – one can't hope to ever completely define – this little bit of heaven on earth.

THE PEOPLE AND THEIR CULTURE. Trying to pin down an accurate, all-encompassing summary of the Irish character and personality is like trying to pin down a butterfly on the wing. Talk about complexity! Just when I think I have them figured out, yet another characteristic crops up to interject, "Yes, but . . ." An anonymous poet came about as close as possible:

> *He's victor and victim, a star and a clod,*
> *He's wild and he's gentle,*
> *He's good and he's bad,*
> *He's proud and he's humble,*
> *He's happy and sad.*
> *He's in love with the ocean, the earth and the skies,*
> *He's enamored with beauty wherever it lies.*
> *He's victor and victim, a star and a clod,*
> *But mostly he's Irish, in love with his God.*

Even *that* doesn't really catch the scope, color, and sheer exuberant nature of these complex people. With my American background, I wonder how Ireland escaped the "melting pot" tag. The people among whom I now live are a fascinating mix of Celt, Viking, Norman, and Saxon blood from invaders who never went home. I see traces of the homelands, however, in an "Irish" race of brunettes, blonds, and redheads. I suppose this mix accounts to some extent for the paradoxical nature of the Irish, but in the end, the collective Irish personality is firmly embedded in Irish individuals – the Seans, Siubhans, Michaels, and Kathleens.

Carriage driver on Inishmore, Aran Islands, County Galway

If I had to compile a list of priorities for most of my Irish friends, religion would probably come first. A staunchly Catholic nation since the fifth century when St. Patrick arrived, Ireland has held fast to the Church, moving from Celtic to Catholic rites without a hitch. For many, life centers around daily attendance at Mass. Nevertheless, in today's Ireland, even though some three million Irish in the Republic and seven hundred thousand in Northern Ireland are Catholic, several Protestant denominations and a small Jewish population are also well represented, and Dublin's small Islamic community worships in its own mosque.

Over the last decade, the Catholic Church's centuries-old grip on the mores and morals of the Irish has begun to loosen, a victim of fast-changing twentieth-century lifestyles. Among my Irish friends are several couples who left broken marriages, and, because divorce is not available to them, are openly living together without benefit of matrimony, a condition unheard of in years gone by, which scarcely raises an eyebrow these days.

If the Irish are anything, they are *friendly*. A simple query for directions can land you at a kitchen table swapping stories over a "cuppa." In bed-and-breakfast homes, the fireside family circle, their friends, and their favorite pub are shared with a warmth I have not found elsewhere. Nor is this generosity of spirit confined to the host family. Over the breakfast table in a Kerry bed-and-breakfast, a lovely Irish lady from Dublin insisted that I be her houseguest when in that city.

There's a panache about the friendly Irish, which I found in Cork City when I asked a total stranger about an address, confessing I was lost. With a broad smile and a sweeping bow that made me laugh, that stranger assured me "You're lost no more, me pet, come with me," and proceeded to escort me to my destination, a steady chatter shortening the walk. Panache!

With all their friendliness, the Irish are anything *but* intrusive. They are quite happy to leave you to your own devices if that is what you want. But ask the first question, make the first comment, or book into a family home as a paying guest—and wholehearted assistance, hospitality, and genuine friendship are your immediate rewards. An American journalist on assignment in Ireland brought his family along, and to his utter amazement, his Irish landlady packed him and his wife off for a week's vacation—without their children, who were by then considered part of her Irish family. Now, *that* is hospitality in its highest form, and it has a terrific side effect: it rubs off on those not born to the culture. Although I now take that sort of friendship and helpfulness for granted, I find myself returning it to strangers, in the Irish way, as well as to my close friends. That is a personal bonus that enriches every day of my life.

It doesn't take long to discover that the Irish are great talkers, positively infatuated with the sound and texture of words. Any Irish man or woman worthy of the name instinctively colors even the most mundane everyday conversation with eloquent, vivid imagery capable of transforming the dullest event into a sometimes wildly fanciful tale. The answer to virtually every question evolves into an entertaining short story. "The craic (talk) was mighty" is a phrase that falls often from Irish lips in describing any gathering that featured lively verbal repartee, and most gatherings do. All that joyous volubility leaps quite readily to the stage and has made the Abbey Theatre and a host of Irish film and stage actors household names around the world.

Running through any conversation is sure to be the celebrated wit of the Irish. More often than not directed at themselves, it is a subtle blend of the skillful use of words and phrases with a fair dash of mischief. It has served the Irish well over long centuries

County Kerry, fishing boats at Knightstown, Ring of Kerry

of foreign rule as both a sly, effective weapon and an emotional release from the cruelties they have endured. Nor is Irish wit any less pointed today, and those who have grandiose ideas of their own importance or who take their personal success too seriously are well advised to watch their backs—the Irish are past masters at deflating egos.

A softer side of Irish humor has caught me unawares from time to time. When I first came to visit, in my innocence it took a while to "cop on" that a canny Irishman, at times tempted beyond resistance by the "stage Irish" image harbored by many visitors, will play the buffoon and act out every known stereotype, in gleeful anticipation of telling the tale to an appreciative audience that night in the local pub. A favorite County Kerry story is that of a young Killarney lad who, on the arrival of warm weather, joyfully puts away his shoes with the announcement. "Sure and isn't it the time to look quaint for the tourists." It takes a bit of insight to spot what is no more than a gentle way of "codding" visitors and sending them away with just what they came looking for. The irony is that the visitors *are* delighted, and they struggle hard to remember verbatim those wonderful Irish words and expressions.

I have developed a theory that much of all that marvelous verbal color and wit is rooted in the ancient Gaelic language. True, English has become the first tongue of the country, but there is no denying that its lilting, melodic tones are uniquely Irish, echoing old Gaelic inflections and structures. According to the Irish, "The English imposed their language on us, but, sure, didn't we show them how to use it." Banished by the British for a time, Gaelic was reinstated as Ireland's official language after the Republic was born and the British left. It shows up in place names, street signs, and government titles. As for its everyday use, more than forty thousand Irish speakers still live in *Gaeltacht* ("Gwale-tack-ta") areas, where English is only spoken occasionally.

Next to talk, music must surely rank highest in the loves of the Irish. Since the early days of their pre-Christian bards, they have been musical—celebrating, commemorating, and lamenting everything in life in song and dance. When Oliver Cromwell attempted to quash Gaelic, the language of all ballads and songs up to that time, the wily Irish used the alien English words to disguise their nationalism by personifying their country as "Roisin Dubh," "Kathleen Huallachain," and "Grainne Uail"—each an ode to Ireland herself and all still very much a part of Ireland's musical life. When British law proscribed the playing of any instrument while on your feet (to prevent bagpipes from leading the rebellious Irish into battle), the *uilleann* (elbow) pipes, which are played sitting down, nicely circumvented that law.

For me, the music of Ireland is one of its most magical and irresistible assets. In country pubs and their plusher city cousins, the concert halls, and at gatherings around family hearths, the melodious harmonies of harp, pipes, *bodhran* (a drum of tightly stretched goatskin), tin whistle, fiddle, and the accordion have broken my heart with one tune, and with the next have sent my feet and spirits flying in joyful, fast-paced jigs and reels. English essayist G. K. Chesterton must have forgotten those jigs and reels when he wrote of the Irish: "All their wars are merry, and all their songs are sad." Still, modern ballads like "The Flight of the Earls," which swept the country when emigration was at its peak in the late 1980s, bring tears to the eyes. Drawing a parallel between the current exodus and a significant historical happening, the lyrics served notice to the country that "those big planes fly both ways" and its youth would be coming back.

County Dublin, stone pier at Dun Laoghaire

Some of my most memorable encounters with all that *craic* and music and general conviviality have been in Ireland's social centers, otherwise known as pubs. Many a wild tale or animated discussion or spontaneous song has broken out over a pint of the creamy-headed Guinness, the country's unofficial national drink. Some of the best stories and songs have emerged in slightly shabby establishments replete with time-worn wood, etched glass, and touches of brass; but others, just as memorable, have erupted in ornate, Victorian-style city watering holes, glitzed-up chrome-and-mirror abysses of pseudo sophistication — and in bare-bones drinking places whose only decor is a gaggle of colorful "regulars."

When they are not talking, singing, or dancing, a fair few of the Irish are writing. This is not surprising, since their literary heritage stretches back to the sixth century, when epic poems and heroic prose passed from ancient bards to monks, who laboriously transcribed them into manuscripts as rich in illustration as they were in language. Gaelic was the dominant language of this literature until the seventeenth century and was widely used up to the beginning of the nineteenth century. When English was imposed, Irish writers found that transferring the richness of their ancient tongue to the foreign language was as simple as tipping the whiskey jug.

The tradition of satire — with works like the Irish-language *Midnight Court,* Brian MacGiolla Meidhre's eighteenth-century account of the Irish male's aversion to marriage — never wavered as it passed on to English-language poets, novelists, dramatists, and short-story writers. Over the centuries, literary greats such as Jonathan Swift, George Bernard Shaw, Sean O'Casey, Oscar Wilde, William Butler Yeats, Edmund Burke, Seamus Heaney, James Joyce, and Patrick Kavanaugh have illuminated the social political, and economic landscape of Ireland with their elegance. And the process continues, with talented writers laboring in relative obscurity to record their unique, very *Irish,* view of the world.

Artists have been equally busy committing an Irish perception to canvas, carrying on a visual arts tradition that stretches back to Newgrange and Bronze Age ornaments and jewelry, whose utilitarian designs were embellished with artistic spirals and mystical symbols. Celtic art also joined hands with literary style in the beautifully illustrated eighth-century *Book of Kells,* which continues to influence modern design. One of my most prized lapel pins is a modern-day adaptation of those designs. Painters Jack B. Yeats (poet W. B.'s brother) and John Lavery earned international recognition, as have contemporary artists Pauline Bewick, James Scanlon, George Campbell, a slew of sculptors, and a growing number of award-winning film makers.

Notwithstanding all those creative indoor pursuits, the Irish are happiest when they are out-of-doors in the midst of their glorious landscape — preferably engaged in a fast-moving hurling or Gaelic football match. Both sports evolved from the days of fierce tribal rivalries when encroaching civilization undoubtedly shoved all that competitive spirit from battleground to football pitch, and both are unique to Ireland. The only thing that can lure a dyed-in-the-wool hurling or football fan from a Sunday afternoon contest is a horse race scheduled at the same time. Irish-bred horses, of course, are highly prized around the globe, and it is a thrilling sight to see them round the last bend of a grass course against a backdrop of mountains or seashore or rolling green fields. The colorful air of a country fair pervades the whole affair. Betting takes on aspects of a sport itself — with bookmakers vying for punters (bettors) while shouting out

County Cork, hay stacks in field on Cape Clear Island

odds that change momentarily – and punters trying to get their bets down when the odds are at their best. That timing, as I learned to my detriment at my first race, is all important, since your winnings are paid (from a big satchel that evokes the carpetbags of American history) at the odds in place when you placed your bet.

The Irish are deeply religious, warm-hearted, witty, occasionally devious, great talkers and even greater listeners, sometimes argumentative to the point of combativeness – and with it all, friendly. How, I have pondered, did they get this way? What explanation can possibly be given for a nature that seems to be so mercurial and paradoxical? The simple answer must be, of course, that these perplexing people have been shaped not only by the staggering beauty of the land in which they live, but also by the extraordinary sequence of events that has landed them in their present circumstances.

THE LAY OF THE LAND. Geologists date native rock back some *twenty-four hundred million* years, fixing the antiquity of the land called Ireland. Over the last six hundred million years, movements of the earth's plates, two glacial Ice Ages, and ancient volcanic eruptions have all played a part in shaping today's landscape. It is thought provoking, indeed, to realize that should the surface of the surrounding seas be lowered by as little as three hundred feet, Ireland would once more become a part of continental Europe.

As it is, this tiny island on the continental shelf west of Great Britain is a jumble of physical features somewhat resembling a lumpy batter stirred by a giant hand that playfully pressed the spoon in the center to create a great depression surrounded by a rim of high ground. Incredibly, that conglomeration of physical features combines to form an island of just 32,524 square miles, 302 miles long and 189 miles wide. The indentations of its jagged, three-thousand-mile-long coastline are so winding that you are never more than seventy miles from the sea; and with more than nine thousand miles of wandering rivers and eight hundred lakes, Ireland is a delightful mix of land and water. When friends come to visit, I know without doubt that at some point during their stay they will exclaim that, in the midst of such ever-changing scenery, it is hard to credit they are traveling in such a small segment of the earth's land mass.

The undulating limestone plain at the center of the island is home to bogs, which have provided peat (invariably called "turf" by the Irish) that have fueled centuries of home fires. Ireland's longest river, the 230-mile-long Shannon, drains much of the area; a network of long, post-glacial river valleys adds magnificent variety; and numerous lakes, large and small, reflect the ever-changing sky. Ringing the central depression, a coastal belt of highlands has led many writers to compare the island's shape to that of a teacup. Superimposed on the geography of the island are ancient political divisions: Connaught, Leinster, Ulster, and Munster.

In the west, the wild topography is a tangled combination of limestone, shale, granite, quartzite, and basalt, which rises to form mountain ranges, then falls away to shelter underground streams, caves, and lakes. It was to this region, during one of Ireland's most tragic episodes, that the Irish were consigned by Oliver Cromwell with the edict "to hell or to Connaught." The bleakness of its landscape ranked the province little better than its alternative. Covering Counties Roscommon, Leitrim, Sligo, Galway, and Mayo, Connaught is a land of rugged coastlines that are overlooked by windswept cliffs and punctuated

County Dublin, horse jumping competition at Dublin Horse Show

by offshore islands; stony inland fields over which loom wild mountains sliced by deep passes; and lake-dotted plains that stretch along the Shannon Valley. This sparsely populated province contains the towns of Galway and Sligo, both of which grew up around river fords.

Ulster still retains its ancient borders, even though Counties Donegal, Monaghan, and Cavin lie in the Republic; the counties of Derry, Antrim, Armagh, Tyrone, Fermanagh, and Down now form the political division of Northern Ireland. One of Ulster's most dominant features – an extensive basaltic plateau – is furrowed by the famed Glens of Antrim, and the magnificent basalt columnar formation known as the Giant's Causeway draws visitors by the thousand to the northern coast. In fact, Ulster's coastline holds some of the country's most spectacular cliff and seascape scenery, ranging from the sheer drop of coastal cliffs to the more gentle heights of the Mountains of Mourne, which "sweep down to the sea" to a gorgeous, curving bay fringed by a wide, golden beach. A land of lakes, Ulster holds Lough Neagh, Ireland's largest, covering some 153 brilliant square miles. The ancient seats of the O'Brien and the princes of Tir Chonaill (the O'Donnells) were in Ulster, and although towns and cities in Ulster are scarce, Derry City, Belfast, and tiny Donegal Town are principal concentrations of population.

It is in the east and south that Ireland displays a lushness quite noticeably missing from the two northern provinces. In the east, Leinster covers a lush and varied landscape that includes the counties of Dublin, Carlow, Laois, Wicklow, Meath, Wexford, Kilkenny, Kildare, Offaly, Westmeath, Longford, and Louth. The Vikings left their mark on the province, founding Dublin in A.D. 988 and expanding Wexford, which was already ancient when Ptolemy marked it on his map in the second century.

Kilkenny, the site of St. Canice's sixth-century cathedral and the one-time capital of the Kingdom of Ossory, bears the stamp of Normans, who invaded in the twelfth century and settled in to stay. In the central limestone plain, midland counties sparkle with myriad lakes and rivers set among boglands that stretch for miles and are an important source of peat for the country's homes and industries. The coastal landscape is composed of curving bays, sandy beaches, and small island nature reserves, with rivers like the Nore and Slaney, in County Kilkenny, cutting through some of the most fertile and heavily wooded countryside in all Ireland.

In the south, Munster sprawls from the east to the west coasts, embracing the counties of Kerry, Limerick, Tipperary, Cork, Clare, and Waterford. The natural divisions of Munster are marked by mountain ranges, rivers, lakes, and the Golden Vale of Tipperary's fertile plain. Around both coasts, lofty cliffs rise above tiny coves and long stretches of sandy beaches. Inland, ancient mountain ranges like the Galtees, Knockmealdowns, Commeraghs, and Slieve Blooms are slashed by deep gaps and scenic passes, while rolling plains are ringed by lush woodlands. At 3,414 feet, Carratuohill in County Kerry claims title as the highest mountain in Ireland. Two of the country's oldest and most important port cities are in Munster: Cork, the largest city in the province, settled in the seventh century by the good St. Finbar; and Waterford founded in 853 by the Vikings. Tiny by comparison to those two cosmopolitan centers, the County Kerry town of Killarney claims top place on the "must see" list for most visitors. Surrounded by island-studded lakes, once havens for dedicated monks from the eleventh to the thirteenth centuries, Killarney drowsed away as a quiet little market village until Englishman Arthur Young happened on its scenic wonders in the

County Clare, country home near Killaloe

eighteenth century and spread the word to a world that has flocked there ever since, transforming it forever into the tourist attraction it is today.

Ireland's coverlet of those celebrated forty shades of green result from warming currents from the Gulf Stream, creating moderate temperatures that range from 70 degrees Fahrenheit to 40 degrees. Add in the frequent showers that come and go (sometimes several in a single day) in the wake of fast-moving weather systems (usually from the west, bringing the heaviest rainfall to western mountains), and you have the perfect setting for Ireland's verdant blanket. Blessed as they are with such a moderate climate, the Irish invariably say of their country, "Ah, sure, it's not too bad – if only it weren't for the weather." I have given up trying to convince them that the weather really isn't that bad. In fact, those showers are, for the most part, a misty, almost ethereal sort of rain that adds an extra dimension to the landscape. Nor is the weather *always* wet – there is sun aplenty from May through August, especially in the "Sunny Southeast" counties of Waterford and Wexford.

Indeed, it is those mild climatic conditions that are continuing to nurture an aggressive reforestation campaign to restore the native tree populations, since oak, ash, and rowan forests – which once covered much of the central plain – had largely disappeared. During the Neolithic Age, huge tracts of land were denuded for cultivation or grazing. Throughout the island, there are now more than four hundred national forests, large plantations of conifers and evergreens, heather-covered bogland, and species of wildflowers found nowhere in the world but County Clare's Burren. Imported exotic trees, plants, and shrubs, one of the few positive legacies of English landlords during the long years of occupation, also go a long way toward regreening a countryside

once stripped of its foliage. Driving across country, I frequently pull into one of the forest areas for the pure joy of its sylvan peace and quiet.

As a nature lover who is afflicted with a deathly fear of wild animals and anything that crawls, I find Ireland a very "user friendly" place to be. Its gorgeous woodlands, bogs, and country-side harbor no life-threatening animal species. True, fossils of several huge mammals dating back to the last Ice Age have been found, but that same period cut Ireland off from continental Europe before snakes could arrive. (Of course, every Irish man, woman, and child knows that the good St. Patrick gets the credit for doing away with the venomous reptile).

Today, it is the harmless hare, stoat, and fox who inhabit the landscape, posing little threat either to people or to a plethora of songbirds, starlings, seabirds, pheasant, quail, mallards, and huge seasonal migrations of bird species. Ireland's rivers and lakes are teeming with bream, dace, pike, perch, and salmon just waiting for the drop of a hook. Along the coast, sea trout, brown trout, bass, whiting, mullet, flounder, plaice, pollack, and coalfish are just a few of the game fish that assure superb deep-sea fishing and seashore angling.

Of all the physical features, the closest to my own heart are Ireland's vast skies, eternally filled with a stunning panoply of scurrying cloud formations that create a delicate shifting of sun and shade on mountainsides, woodlands, bogs, and fertile fields. When I walk through the brilliance of an Irish sunset, or am stopped by the beauty of stone-walled fields that shade in a mat-ter of seconds from dull grey to bright, shining green, or wonder at the luminosity of a misty "soft day," I am aware of the many dimensions of the physical world in which I now live. George Bernard Shaw must have felt much the same when he wrote:

County Donegal, fisherman and kelp piles, near Halin Head

There is no magic like that of Ireland.
There are no skies like Irish skies.
There is no air like Irish air . . .
The Irish climate will make the stiffest
and slowest mind flexible for life.

Springing from such a wondrous landscape, the Irish seem to come into the world with a deep love for their land, a love that colors every facet of their complex personality. Though not born to it, I realize that, as it has shaped the people with whom I share it, the physical face of this ancient land is slowly and surely shaping me, broadening my thoughts, lengthening my vision, tuning me to the timeless rhythms of earth, sea, and sky.

THE HISTORY. If there is anything Ireland has plenty of, it is history. Every bend of every road, every stone and every bush has a story to tell, and nine times out of ten, there is someone at hand to recount, as vividly as if they happened yesterday, the tales of long ago.

The character of today's Irish is haunted by Stone Age ghosts who peer from the mists of prehistory; by wraiths of the Bronze Age who inhabit a reconstructed crannog at Craggaunowen in County Clare; by spectral sounds, just beyond your ears, of those sheltered in Iron Age forts; by early Christian spirits who left behind great monastic crosses, ruined abbeys, and tower refuges against the Viking raiders; by echoing footsteps of the Vikings in the streets of Dublin and Waterford; by Norman spirits roaming ruined castles that crown the most desirable and fertile bits of Ireland's landscape.

In post-Ice Age Ireland, a land bridge connected its east coast to Great Britain. Stone Age settlers crossed over to Ireland around 6000 B.C. and settled along the coast and the banks of the major inland rivers, using crude tools for fishing and hunting. The land link eventually disappeared, making Ireland an island. It was around 2000 B.C. that a wave of Neolithic settlers arrived, bringing domestic animals and initiating farming and cattle raising as they cleared land and planted crops. Cremation was a part of their culture, and it was they who left behind those communal burial chambers beneath stone cairns or inside earthen, tunnel-filled mounds (such as one-square-mile Newgrange in County Meath) that are such prominent features of the landscape.

All the while, on the continent, metal-working clans were evolving. It was their search for copper to make bronze tools and weapons, and gold to fashion exquisite ornaments that brought them to Ireland's rich deposits. The Bronze Age was underway, and it instigated a virtual invasion of this remote, primitive little island by artisans and merchants who, with Ireland as their home base, peddled their crafts across continental Europe.

Short, dark-haired, and swarthy-skinned, the newcomers are thought to have been Picts of Mediterranean origin. Although the Romans knew them as "Iberni," their name in Ireland became "Uib-Ernai." Ireland's name, the oldest national name in the world, is their legacy; they claimed descendence from the fertility goddess *Eire*, whose name translates as "noble."

Perhaps their most important legacy, however, is the wealth of stone structures testifying to their scientific knowledge and engineering skills. These megaliths also speak silently of the superb organization of a work force of hundreds and an incredible sense of dedication.

Then came the Celts. Tall, with fair complexions and fiery red hair, they migrated to Ireland in the fourth century B.C. after centuries of roaming throughout Europe. Along with their

County Donegal, Lough Veagh, near Glenveagh Castle

24

fierce, warlike nature and military expertise, they brought their language and iron weapons, a potent factor in establishing them as rulers of the land. Small territorial kingdoms were marked out by chieftains of some one hundred clans, and each, in turn, came under the rule of regional kings, who presided over Ulster, Munster, Leinster, Meath, and Connaught. In time, the Kingdom of Meath merged with Leinster, and the Hill of Tara became the seat of the High King.

The High Kings wore precarious crowns, for the hot-blooded Celtic nature bred great battles as petty king fought petty king, and regional kings fought to enlarge their boundaries. Within the hierarchy, most peasants and craftsmen were bound to the chieftain in power at the moment; even "free" farmers anted up both tribute and loyalty. Although all theoretically enjoyed the protection of their overlords, shrewd farmers living away from the seats of power depended on earthen ring forts to protect them from surprise raids by roaming marauders. Today, "rath" or "lis" in a town's name is an indication that there is an ancient ring fort nearby.

Despite the in-fighting, the strong bonds of common culture, traditions, and language created a certain unity between clans. Traditional Brehon law was, in many cases, more just than modern legislation (for instance, women were guaranteed far more rights and equality than in today's world) and demanded a strict adherence that cut across clan lines. Great honor and rich rewards followed bards who traveled from kingdom to kingdom, reciting long, epic poems of heroic deeds of the past as well as the latest exploits of their host chieftain. These minstrel-poets preserved Irish history long before monks wrote it down. Schools of learning with graded scales of achievement were established by scholars and professional people. And welcomed

at each chieftain's table were the artisans and craftsmen of his clan. Druids, who conducted or prescribed sacred ceremonies, were heralded as all clans' wisest men.

All that history and pre-history is fascinating enough as told by historians and archeologists, who base their account of how things happened on such things as artifacts, carbon datings, and educated guesses. But the Irish themselves, world-champion embellishers, have a whole cornucopia of flamboyant legends to enliven virtually every part of the tale. How much exaggeration and color has been added as tales passed down from those early bards to the *seanachies* (storytellers) of today is anybody's guess. But one thing is certain – their delightful blend of fact, fantasy, and mysticism has nothing whatever to do with carbon dating.

They tell of "men of the quiver" *(Fir Bolg)*, "men of the territory" *(Fir Domhnann)*, and "men of Gaul" *(Fir Gaileoin)*. These, claims an ancient legend, were the three original racial groups in early Ireland. Then there are the magical *Tuatha de Danaan*, who went underground to become the "little people" in Ireland's fairy forts. The *seanachies*, in a fit of revisionist history, even came up with a rationale for the shared traits of Irish and Scottish Celts. All were, they reckoned, descended from one man, Mileadh (Milesius), and could look back in their lineage to one Gadelius and a lady known as Scota.

Heroic deeds by heroic men and women such as Conaire Mor, King of Ireland in the second century B.C. are told and retold. A giant in deed as well as size, the much-loved Finn MacCool led his faithful Fianna warrior band to everlasting glory with unmatched feats of bravery and daring, as when they battled to defeat the King of the World at Ventry on the Dingle Peninsula. Homesickness was the downfall of Oisin, one of Finn's Fianna, who enjoyed a magical sojourn in the underground Land of Youth

County Galway, harbor at village of Roundstone

and only succumbed to old age during a visit to his earthly home. In the north, Knights of the Red Branch and courageous Cuchulainn's heroic death (tied to a stone so he would die on his feet when overcome by superior forces) weave a tapestry of valiant men and unassailable honor. As heroic as their menfolk, Queen Maeve of Connaught and the tragic Deirdre of the Sorrows hold top honors among the heroines of song and story, and Irish children still grieve over the enchanted Children of Lir, who were condemned to a centuries-long life as swans.

Where lies the truth, with archeologists or the *seanachies?* Take your pick. Among my Irish friends, these marvelous tales and those who people them are as fresh in their minds and hearts as when their ancestors first listened raptly to the bards of old. As for me, I *do* give due credence to historians and archeologists, but I must confess to a decided prejudice toward Finn MacCool and Cuchulainn. Ireland makes it easy to believe in magic.

In 432 A.D., these were the barbarous, warring people with a highly developed culture who welcomed Christianity in the person of St. Patrick. Born a Roman, St. Patrick came to Ireland as a youthful slave who tended swine in Ulster. When he escaped and returned to the continent, he entered religious life and later returned to Ireland as a missionary. The insight into native Irish life gleaned during those years as a slave served him well in his missionary campaign. Knowing full well the hostility he would arouse by debunking completely their cherished pagan beliefs, he kept just enough of their traditional rites and superstitions to serve as a fertile soil in which to plant Christianity. Many a Christian "holy well" has usurped its healing powers from the ancient Celts. In recognition of the Celtic love of the mystical in nature, he turned to the native shamrock as a symbol of the Holy Trinity. So easy did the good saint make the transition for the Irish that their centuries-old pagan religion embraced the doctrines and rites of Christianity with hardly a ripple on the waters of Irish life.

The conversion of the Irish chieftains was an important new development in the country's history. Although the Celtic natures held on to the old traditions of warfare and unbridled revelry at court, the clan chieftains rushed to pay homage to the new religion through lavish gifts of land for monastic buildings, precious metals, and – most important – the protection of the Christian leaders. With their tradition of reverence for higher education, hundreds of Irish Celts rushed to the monastic universities for a cloistered life of learning that embraced all the knowledge of their time, both Celtic and Roman. They were joined by thousands of Europeans who were fleeing the continent's bleak Dark Ages. Single-handedly, these great universities kept alive most of the known sciences, theology, philosophy, astronomy, literature, and poetry. Gradually, Ireland became the western world's center of learning, the "Land of Saints and Scholars." Its Golden Age was the only lamp of knowledge still alight in the western world during the seventh and eighth centuries. The high artistic achievement of that age is epitomized by the exquisitely illustrated *Book of Kells.*

While all this was going on, seventh-century monks of another ilk headed for more remote parts of the country and to rocky islands just offshore. Following a lifestyle of severe austerity, they lived in unique, beehive-shaped stone huts that have survived the centuries.

By the end of the eighth century, the returning scholars and Irish missionaries relit the flame of education on the continent by establishing great European universities and reintroducing arts and sciences to royal courts and cathedrals.

Pastureland near Newcastle, County Down

But the wealth of the monastic settlements of Ireland had not gone unnoticed. In A.D. 795 fierce bands of Vikings landed along the coastline and, flaunting their superior mail battle dress and heavy arms, launched terrifying raids, plundering and taking captives. As they moved inland, the distinctly Irish, tall, round towers, with access only by retractable ladders to entrances high aboveground, became depositories of Ireland's most precious treasures. With a twinkle of the eye, the Irish insist that it was really Finn MacCool who built the first of these and that the doorway was simply put at his natural entry-level. Later monks, the legend says, just recognized the design as a perfect protective device.

Gradually, Ireland worked its magic on the raiders, and they became the first in a long string of invaders who settled down, intermarried with the natives, and were "more Irish than the Irish." Dublin became their first permanent settlement, quickly followed by the coastal towns of Wexford, Waterford, Cork, and Limerick, and to this day their presence may be felt in surviving bits of city walls, gates, and fortifications like Waterford's remarkably intact Reginald's Tower.

Irish chieftains were not inclined to relinquish power to each other, let alone foreign invaders. After adopting the Vikings' battle methods, in 1014 the High King of Ireland, Brian Boru took them on at Clontarf, just outside Dublin. After a full day of battle, the great Irish leader won a decisive victory, but suffered mortal wounds in the process.

For a century and a half after Brian Boru's death, the Irish chieftains continued to engage in their time-honored tug-of-war to establish one single central authority figure. And it was one of those ambitious combatants who took the first step leading to the country's centuries-long involvement with the British. Dermot MacMurrough, King of Leinster, during a respite from battle, made the fatal mistake of stealing chieftain O'Rourke's beautiful wife. The aggrieved King of Brefni promptly enlisted the aid of a number of minor chieftains to hound MacMurrough out of Leinster. Then Irish history took yet another turn, for it was the enmity of these two leaders that led to Ireland's first encounter with her next invaders.

MacMurrough turned to the Norman King Henry II, who then ruled England, and persuaded him to raise an army to fight for MacMurrough's lost kingdom. Led by the Earl of Pembroke ("Strongbow"), the Norman invaders landed in Waterford in 1169, and their wily leader scored a coup by marrying MacMurrough's daughter, thus assuming the title of King of Leinster on the death of her father in 1170. Moving out to gain domination over most of Leinster and Munster, Strongbow defeated Rory O'Connor, the last High King of Ireland, and became so powerful that King Henry II sat up and took notice.

Under the guise of a religious reformer, Henry descended on Ireland brandishing a decree from Pope Adrian IV, the only English pope in the Church's history, granting him lordship over all lands and inhabitants of Ireland, and thus over Strongbow. With this lever, he was able to elicit the fealty of Strongbow and the Irish kings, lords, and large landowners by renting or granting lands and titles only to those who professed loyalty to the Crown. It was the beginning of a practice that would last for centuries, as chieftains schemed to hold their territories by giving lip service to the English king while maintaining their own loyalties in silence.

For the next 350 years, Norman and Irish lords vied for the land-granting favor of the successive English monarchs. Occupied by civil wars and foreign conquests, English rulers paid

County Antrim, Dunluce Castle and north coast cliffs

little attention to the antics across the Irish Sea, and Normans managed to acquire more than half the country, spreading a plethora of sturdy castles across the landscape.

The Normans, however, proved to be as vulnerable to Ireland's spell as their predecessors, the Vikings. Still professing their English origins, their intermarriage with the Irish and their adaptation to native culture created an Anglo-Irish group so highly visible that once more the English throne felt a threat. To call a halt to this straying from all things English, Parliament passed laws against their use of Irish dress and manners, and — perhaps for the first time in the world's history — banned the use of the native language. But by this time, primary Anglo-Irish loyalties were to their own Irish land holdings — the English Crown came a poor second.

In the meantime, Irish chieftains and kings who had refused to play the lip-service game and had lost their lands waged incessant warfare to regain them. The trouble was that each battled independently, with no central organization or authority, and their efforts only resulted in concentrating beleaguered English Crown forces in a heavily fortified area around Dublin, known as "The Pale," and in a few scattered garrison towns. As things stood, it seemed quite possible to the English that the Irish might manage to regain total control of their ancient land. Something had to be done, and in 1541, King Henry VIII broke with Rome, threw out the papal decree, proclaimed himself King of Ireland by right of conquest, declared all opposition as rebellion, and set about dispossessing Irish and Anglo-Irish rebel leaders and replacing them with more loyal subjects.

Unfortunately for the English monarchy, the Catholic religion survived (albeit underground) the demise of the papal decree. When Elizabeth became queen, measures meant to enforce the

Reformation in Ireland inspired the staunchly Catholic Irish to fight for their religion even more fervently than they had for their lands. Resisting the pull of higher education, they refused to renounce their church to enter Trinity College, which Elizabeth established for Protestants to "win the Papists away from cant and superstition." Uprising after uprising failed before superior British forces, and in 1601, Irish leaders appealed to Spain for help. The plan was to make a decisive stand at Kinsale in County Cork, where Spanish and Irish forces occupied the town. But Kinsale was surrounded by English troops, and Irish hopes now lay with two northern chieftains, The O'Neill and The O'Donnell. Those two stalwarts embarked on an epic winter march designed to surprise the British from behind. They might have succeeded had not the British got wind of the Irish tactics — rumors still persist that it was a drunken Irish soldier captured by the British who tipped them off. Forewarned, the British won the day, sending the best of the chieftains into hiding. By 1608, the last of the Irish leaders set sail from northern Ireland for the continent, leaving behind their confiscated lands, which had been handed over to English and Scottish settlers.

The "Flight of the Earls" left the Irish bereft of any organized resistance to English rule, and they turned to harassment, with a series of bloody attacks that were met with the inevitable bloody reprisals. In 1641, they embarked on an ambitious plan to retake the lands of Ulster, which resulted in the arrival of the Puritan general Oliver Cromwell in 1649, ushering in perhaps the most savage period of Irish history.

A religious fanatic as well as astute politician, Cromwell began his campaign at Drogheda, brutally slaying more than thirty thousand Irish men, women, and children. Cutting a horrifying swathe of blood across the country, he left churches, castles,

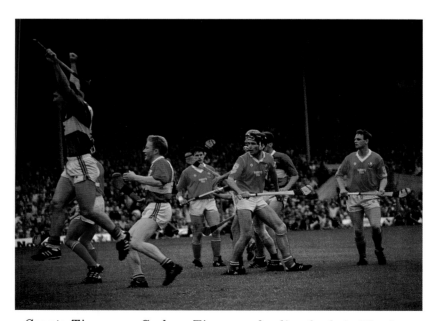

County Tipperary, Cork vs. Tipperary hurling finals in Thurles

and homes in ruins. Those Irish who escaped the sword were consigned to the hell of slave labor in tropical English sugar plantations or driven to bleak, stone-strewn Connaught. The most fertile Irish landholdings served as rewards to Cromwell's officers, and in the end, less than one-ninth of Irish soil remained in the hands of natives.

In 1688, the Catholic King James II came to the throne, only to be quickly deposed by William of Orange. When James sought refuge in Ireland in 1689, the Irish flocked to his support. Taking up arms, they laid siege to those Ulster cities that harbored Protestants loyal to William, only to face total defeat at the hands of "King Billy" at the Battle of the Boyne in 1690. The luckless James deserted his Irish supporters, who fought on under Patrick Sarsfield until October of 1691. That conflict was ended by the infamous Treaty of Limerick, which purported to guarantee the Irish both their religion and their land.

To this day, however, Limerick is known as the City of the Violated Treaty, for Parliament not only refused to ratify the treaty, but went much further in passing the oppressive Penal Laws. All civil and political rights were denied to Catholics. They were forbidden to vote or hold public office; enter any of the professions, especially law; educate their children; own a horse valued at more than £5; bear arms; or leave their land to only one son, being required instead to divide it into smaller plots for all male heirs, thus setting the pattern for Ireland's tiny farmlands of today. In exchange for the privilege of living in crude huts and raising a small plot of potatoes to keep their families from starving, Irish farmers working on the estates of absentee English landlords paid exorbitant rents. This sorry state of affairs for the proud descendants of heroic kings and chieftains lasted through a full century. It was a century that spawned illegal "hedge schools" and the celebration of Mass in secluded mountains and glens, as the Irish struggled to save their culture and religion from oblivion.

During those years, Anglo-Irish Protestants transferred their strongest allegiance from England to Ireland in ever-increasing numbers, and in the late 1700s, the Protestant Patriot party, led by Henry Grattan, demanded greater independence. Although the 1782 Irish Parliament that sat in Dublin (under the tight control of London) was no more than a token gesture to the independence of Ireland, it did gradually relax Penal Laws and increase trade between Ireland and England. Dublin flourished, with a lively social life and streets lined with Georgian mansions and gracious squares.

That taste of independence—never mind that it was a very *limited* taste—served only to whet the appetite of a group of Irishmen who were led by Wolfe Tone. In 1791, he formed the Society of United Irishmen, a union of Catholics and Protestants dedicated to a *totally* independent Irish republic. Turning to a newly established republic in France for military aid, Tone plotted a 1798 insurrection that ended in pure disaster and gave the British rulers a potent weapon for ending even the limited Irish parliamentary rule that had existed. The 1800 Act of Union was passed, which English logic reckoned would put Ireland in her proper place—again. Of course, they were dead wrong, and in 1803, Robert Emmet launched yet another uprising. It was the same old story, however, and ended with Emmet gallantly declaring from the gallows, "When my country takes her place among the nations of the earth, then, and not till then, let my epitaph be written."

On the political front, a young Catholic by the name of Daniel O'Connell was elected in 1828 to the English Parliament and

County Clare, crab hunting on beach in town of Lahinch

promptly started to make noises about Catholic Emancipation – a total repeal of the Penal Laws, and the restoration of all Catholic civil rights. Spurred on by the success of that campaign the following year, he waged battle for repeal of the Act of Union, earning a place in Irish hearts and the title of "The Liberator." The Young Ireland movement was just beginning when tragedy struck from a different quarter, and once more the Irish goal became one of sheer survival.

A disastrous potato blight spread throughout the country in 1846, destroyed the basic food supply of Irish peasantry, and brought with it the onslaught of a devastating famine. Relief efforts were pitifully ineffective, especially since British ships continued to sail to England laden with cargoes of Irish-grown grain and other crops. Entire Irish families were wiped out by starvation or by the plague that followed on its heels, and during the next three years, a population of nearly nine million native Irish was reduced to a little over six million. Landlords continued to demand exorbitant rents from tenants, evicting hundreds of thousands who could not pay. Roadside ditches, filled with emaciated bodies of these displaced people, became a common sight. Of those who survived, more than a million set out for the United States and Canada on overcrowded, filthy, disease-infested ships that were little more than floating coffins.

When the famine finally lifted, the Irish tenant-farmers, who remembered the harsh rule of the British landlords during the period of suffering, eagerly joined with Charles Stewart Parnell and Michael Davitt in 1879 to form the Land League, which was dedicated to fighting the oppressive land rentals. All around the country, the Land Leaguers struck back at landlords who evicted tenants by the simple, but deadly effective, method of shunning their families and cutting off all services. Their first target was a County Mayo landlord, Captain Boycott, whose name became synonymous with the tactic. Not surprisingly, rents came down to reasonable levels, and tenants enjoyed some protection against eviction, as well as – eventually – the right to purchase their own land.

But the Land League was only an interim step for the Irish in their unfailing zeal for freedom from English rule. An energetic campaign for limited independence was led for many years by Charles Stewart Parnell. As England teetered on the brink of World War I, Home Rule was finally granted by Parliament, over strong opposition from loyal Ulster Unionists and Protestants determined to keep Ireland a part of England. A minority in the largely Catholic population, they declared that Home Rule equated to Rome Rule.

Once more, the country fairly bristled with guns as the loyalist Ulster Volunteers armed to combat the equally determined Irish Republican Army, the military arm of the republican political party Sinn Fein ("shin fain"), whose name means "ourselves alone." At first, this ugly domestic conflict was put on the back burner as world conflict of enormous magnitude erupted.

On Easter Monday of 1916, however, "the Irish question," as the British termed Ireland's fight for Irish independence, moved back to a very *hot* front burner. Much to the surprise of most of the Irish people, Patrick Pearse and James Connolly led a poorly armed band of fewer than two hundred up Dublin's O'Connell Street to the General Post Office. In the name of a Provisional Government, they occupied the impressive building, and Pearse stood between the front pillars to read in ringing tones "The Proclamation of the Irish Republic to the People of Ireland." The valiant little band dug in and prepared to stand their ground as long as it might be humanly possible.

Tidal flats near Cruit Island, County Donegal

Under constant bombardment, they held the building for six days under the banner of Ireland's ancient symbol, a golden harp on a pennant of brilliant green, and the Sinn Fein banner of green, white, and orange. All told, fewer than one thousand joined in the rebellion, but the remarkable courage they displayed in the face of overwhelming British military might entered the annals of Ireland's heroic legends. When surrender proved inevitable, Post Office survivors marched back down O'Connell Street under British guns, their heads bloodied but unbowed. The entire country watched and waited to learn their fate.

It was only when Pearse, Connolly, and fourteen others were executed by firing squad and hundreds were imprisoned or exiled that Irish loyalties finally united. World opinion was stirred by the ideal of Irish independence, and as the patriots fell in Kilmainham Gaol's courtyard, William Butler Yeats tragically proclaimed that "a terrible beauty is born."

From 1916 to 1921, Britain struggled against a rebellion that simply refused to die with its leaders. They sent mercenaries known as the Black and Tans to roam the Irish countryside, terrorizing innocent citizens as well as rebels, but the resistance only increased. In 1919, guerrilla warfare – replete with atrocities, ambush tactics, and assassinations – became the norm after Sinn Fein won a huge majority of parliamentary seats and refused to go to London, setting up a National Parliament of Ireland in Dublin.

Then, in December of 1921, after two years of bloodshed, the Anglo-Irish Treaty was signed, establishing an Irish Free State of twenty-six counties. As an integral part of the British Empire, it was to follow the same self-governing pattern of the other British dominions. Because of their loyalist sympathies, six counties in Ulster would remain under rule from London.

Instead of bringing peace, the treaty became the focus for further armed struggle. Civil war raged until 1923 as Eamon de Valera led the Irish Republican party in their fight to include all thirty-two counties in the Irish Republic, which they believed they had fought for all along. William Cosgrave and the newly formed government, on the other hand, felt that the treaty terms were acceptable for the moment and that in time the six counties of Northern Ireland would join the other twenty-six by constitutional means. Thus was cast the first shadow of a division that haunts Ireland today.

When the futility of continued civil conflict became obvious, de Valera ceased hostilities and founded the Fianna Fail ("feena foil") party, which came to power in 1932, finally abolishing the oath of allegiance to the Crown. It was not until 1948, however, that Great Britain formally declared Ireland independent and outside the Commonwealth. Ireland's coalition government, led by John A. Costello, proudly declared, "the description of the State shall be the Republic of Ireland."

Political events in Northern Ireland since its separation from the Republic weave a tangled web that would baffle the judgment of a Solomon. The province has evolved into an environment in which violence emerges as the perceived remedy for all of the injustices of the past and present. The Catholic minority, after suffering decades of religious discrimination, has a deep yearning for a united Ireland that permeates every aspect of daily life. Across a deep emotional divide, Protestants fear any change in a privileged status quo based on centuries of firmly rooted family history and answer violence with violence. Everyday life goes on, with segregated populations keeping a wary eye on each other as they pursue their livelihoods and strive for an atmosphere in which to raise their families in peace and safety.

County Kerry, low tide along harbor wall at Portmagee

To those ends, the Civil Rights movement of 1968 generated both hope and fear, but when the British army arrived to quell the "troubles," the situation deteriorated. The Northern Ireland Assembly of 1973, the Women's Peace Movement of 1976, the Anglo-Irish Agreement of 1986, and the on-going conferences involving leading Northern Ireland political parties and both the British and Irish governments have made advances, but a peaceful Ireland has proved elusive. Meanwhile, Irish men and women on both sides of the border hold a steadfast belief in a future that will see reconciliation and justice on all sides.

South of the border, the Irish engage in politics with the same relish with which their chieftains long ago approached those ancient inter-clan skirmishes – and with such flair that I sometimes think, while watching the evening news on television, that I should really should be paying an entertainment tax. Political parties split to form splinter groups, and governments rise and fall as the articulate Irish public puts its collective foot down at any governmental skullduggery, avarice, or – deadly sin – arrogance. At present, this tiny country sports no less than six very active political parties, and in its less-than-a-century existence as an independent nation, has seen some twenty-seven governments, the majority of them coalitions between the two largest parties and varying lesser parties. Yet, somehow, all those combinations have managed to develop firm policies of military neutrality, membership in the United Nations, and alliance with the European Community.

Ireland is, however, a country in the throes of social, political, and economic transition. One symbol of this was the 1990 election, which placed in office Ireland's first woman president, the eloquent Mary Robinson. Small farms still flourish, but agriculture is becoming less prominent as international service and high-tech industries are attracted by a clean environment, tax incentives, and an educated, work-oriented population. A by-product of that influx is the birth of domestic firms supplying raw materials and information to foreign-owned companies. The growing tourism industry is based on Ireland's character and its natural beauties and ancient relics – an echo of its historic role as host to visitors, welcomed and unwelcomed.

In the wake of these changes, the youthful population is shifting from rural areas to the cities. Although the severe world-wide recession in the 1980s sent Irish youth abroad in search of work, the 1990s have seen a gradual return of the emigrants, creating alarming unemployment figures that are the country's most pressing problem.

No matter what difficulties might lie ahead, the longer I live here, the more aware I am of an almost tangible aura of timelessness overlying the whole of Ireland. It is as though this land has endured since the beginning of time and will be here until time has come to an end. All the details of modern life are played out against a backdrop of pre-historic ruins and the crumbling remains of castles and towers – all wearing the soft patina of the centuries. There they sit, unattended and devoid of the neon-sign, souvenir-stand environment of the historical sites of my home country. Left in the wake of tumultuous – often devastating – events, they harmonize so perfectly with their settings of green fields and rocky hilltops that they seem to merge gracefully into the landscape. Nothing wrought by the hand of man in the years to come, I think, can ever drastically change this enchanting, *enduring* little country. Timeless.

Right: In the far north is County Donegal's rugged landscape, with its foundations of cave-riddled limestone and strangely beautiful rocks.

County Antrim, town of Portbradden

◄ Reminders of long-ago Irish peasant life remain along Donegal's heavily indented coast and among inland rocky flats, great mountains, and deep glens. From small cottages come the beautiful, nubby, hand-woven tweeds and woolens, whose earth colors come from traditional vegetable dyes.
▲ Donegal's history is traced in great houses, castles, fortifications, and villages that followed English plantations.

▲ Killybegs, in County Donegal, is one of the most important commercial fishing ports in Ireland. Not to be missed by the visitor is the late afternoon arrival of the fishing fleet, with half the town gathered to meet the returning mariners.
► The cliffs of Slieve League, said to be Europe's tallest, rise some eighteen hundred feet on Donegal's craggy coast.

◄ Between the cliffs and mountain ranges, great, curving
sandy beaches embroider the coastline of County Donegal.
▲ Trowbreaga Bay is near Malin Head, the northernmost
point of mainland Ireland. Malin Head is one of the peninsulas
that stretch the coastline to more than three thousand miles.
►► The vastness of her skies matches the shining breadth of
Ireland's surrounding seas, the Atlantic and the Irish Sea.

▲ A proud resident of County Mayo's Clare Island admires the gravestone of his home's most illustrious citizen, the sixteenth-century sea queen, Grainneuaile (Grace O'Malley), whose feats of warfare and piracy are legendary and still recounted with much gusto. The indomitable Irishwoman astonished Elizabeth I by declaring that she could not, in all conscience, bow to the English queen, since "We are equals — in my own place I am as much sovereign as you in yours."

▲ County Mayo skies look down on wonderful landscapes of varied beauty featuring mountains, plains, moorlands, offshore islands, and islet-studded lakes and bays, often under the canopy of a spectacular rainbow. Among County Mayo's most prominent attractions is the holy mountain of Croagh Patrick, where, in 441, St. Patrick spent the forty days of Lent in prayer. This event is commemorated each year when thousands join a national pilgrimage on the last Sunday in July.

▲ Artists have long felt the frustration of trying to depict the light of the Irish heavens. The delicate play of sun and shade over mountain passes, the mistiness of a "soft" day, the swirling blackness of storm clouds, the feathery white clouds scudding across a background of purest blue, the fantastic ruby-red glow of sunset over County Donegal's Bloody Foreland – all try the very souls of those who would attempt to commit them to canvas, film, or the printed page.

▲ The Irish zealously nurture a religious ferver developed over centuries. There are countless holy days, collective pilgrimages and purely personal tributes to saints, holy wells, and religious relics. Not even the prospect of a slogging ascent, sometimes in bare feet, up the slopes of Croagh Patrick dims the enthusiasm of a people who have managed to seamlessly weave pagan customs into Christian rituals.

▲ Movements in the earth's plates account for Ireland's great limestone plain – which geologists say was formed as long ago as five hundred million years – and the throwing up of cliffs and flat-topped hills rising as high as two thousand feet above the limestone blocks in County Sligo. The best-known, Ben Bulben, was much loved by poet William Butler Yeats, who lived many years "Under bare Ben Bulben's head."

▲ The undisputed hub of local social life, Irish pubs come in all shapes, sizes, and decors. Acknowledged as "the poor man's university," pub life is governed by pub etiquette, a delicate and complex matter best absorbed over a well-pulled pint of Guinness. There was a trend a few years ago toward chrome and plastic, but pubs like this one in County Mayo are restoring or preserving traditional fronts, snugs, and etched glass.

▲ Several of Ireland's ancient — and not so ancient — castles have metamorphosed into posh luxury hotels. One of the first, and still one of the most popular, is Ashford Castle, just outside Cong in County Mayo. The keep of the original castle, built in 1228, is now incorporated into a slightly eccentric conglomeration of widely varied architectural styles.
▶ Benedictine nuns in the magnificient Kylemore Abbey in County Galway observe vespers in the abbey's chapel.

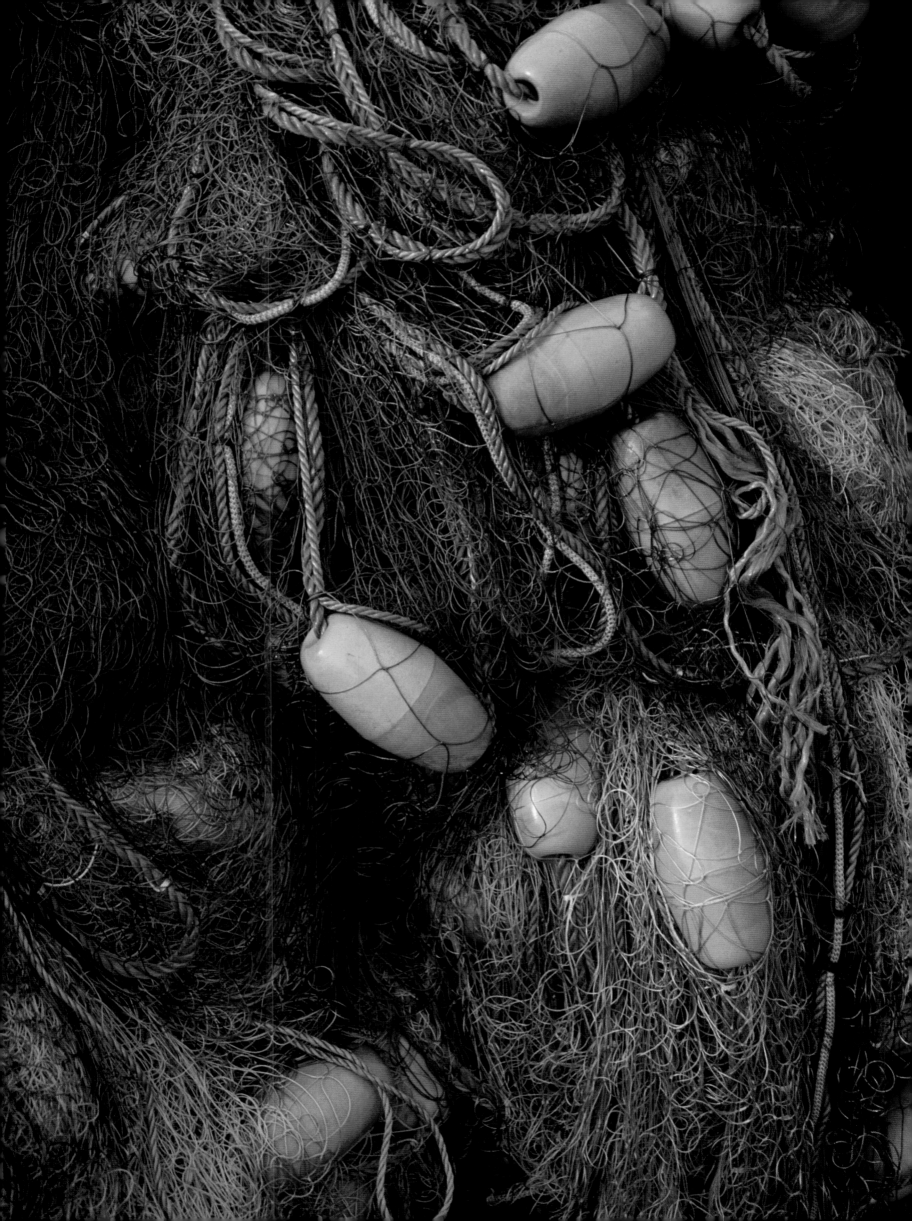

◄ In County Galway's Connemara region, fishermen spread their nets in colorful display on the docks of the village of Roundstone. They continue an occupation begun in this land of stony beauty by nineteenth-century Scottish settlers.
▲ In Cill Ronain (Kilronan) harbor on Inishmore, largest of the three Aran Islands off the Galway coast, ancient relics and modern vessels reflect the area's seafaring heritage.

▲ Undisturbed by walkers, cyclists, or buggies, donkeys – a familiar sight on Inishmore – relax in a peaceful environment.
► In their never-ceasing struggle for self-sufficiency in that barren landscape, the hardy islanders on Inishmaan, the second largest of the Aran Island group, have created small, stone-enclosed fields of tillable ground, composed of sand, shells, and seaweed, all gathered by back-breaking effort.

◄ Irish family life exhibits little generation gap. Parents are involved in their offsprings' activities, and even teenagers often happily shepherd along their younger siblings.
▲ Fishing boats tie up at Galway's docks on a misty morning, as do much larger cargo vessels from around the world.
►► Gorse casts its golden hue against a background of green along the shores of Lake Derravaragh in County Westmeath.

▲ In Dublin, Trinity College's Old Library's lofty, vaulted Long Room is truly awe-inspiring. Lined with marble busts of Ireland's famous figures, it holds glass cases displaying the magnificently illustrated *Book of Kells*. The ancient manuscript, handwritten by monks in Latin, is a priceless link with Ireland's antiquity. Each day a different page is on display.
▶ Dublin's Georgian doors are a trademark of the city. Their elaborate knockers often depict figures from mythology.

◄ This Dublin street market vies for the business of late shoppers, as bright lights switch on and dusk begins to fall.
▲ ▲ Dressed in his best bib and tucker, this judge takes a rest as he surveys the fine Irish horses at the Dublin Horse Show.
▲ County-wide jumping teams parade for the packed stands before the competition begins at the Dublin Horse Show.

▲ ▲ Car ferries daily make the run between Dun Laoghaire, or "Dun Leary" pier, and Holyhead in the United Kingdom.
▲ At the Dun Laoghaire ferry pier, the Aer Lingus Pipe Band plays a musical tribute to transportation by sea and air.
► A 1796 masterpiece of the famed architect, James Gandon, Dublin's famous Four Courts underwent a fierce, two-month Civil War siege in 1922. The subsequent fire spread to the nearby Public Records Office and destroyed its contents.

◄ With more than a thousand pubs from which to chose, these Dublin businessmen have landed at the much-loved, traditional Doheny & Nesbitts, where a beveled mirror in the back lounge reflects the multiple image of a convivial patron.
▲ Dubliners no longer pay the ha'penny toll exacted in 1821 from people setting off across the newly erected cast-iron Halfpenny Bridge, the city's only footpath across the Liffey.

▲ It is from street hawkers in Moore Street Market that the unique accents and rhythms, along with the rich vocabulary, of "Dublin in the Rare Auld Times" are heard. Horse-drawn carts are still very much in evidence along Moore Street.
▶ Ireland's principal port, Dublin is blessed with a broad, deep harbor whose docks extend up the Liffey into the city.

◄ Accustomed to frequent rain, the Irish cherish each day of
sunshine, and many will stop on city streets to relish the
golden glow reflected by Dublin buildings, like this one, the
Sunlight Chambers on Parliament Street, beside the Liffey.
▲ An original circular keep is the only survivor of rebuilding
in the eighteenth century that changed Dublin Castle's out-
ward appearance. During Ireland's 1992 presidency of the
European Community, the interior was completely restored.

▲ Trinity College admitted Protestants only for many years
after it was founded in 1591, but today's students are drawn
from all religions and every social strata and walk of life.
► Nowhere is architecture of Georgian Dublin more striking
than in townhouses and mansions lining Fitzwilliam Square.
► ► Dubliners take a rainy night in stride and would never
cancel a stroll down Grafton Street because of the weather.

◄ Powerscourt Estate and Gardens, perched on high ground near Enniskerry in County Wicklow, is set in a fourteen-thousand-acre demesne. Views of Great Sugarloaf Mountain provide dramatic contrast to Japanese and Italian gardens, including a vast array of rare shrubs and a lovely waterfall.

▲ Rowing is a popular sport in Ireland, and Wicklow Town residents turn out in great numbers for the annual regatta.

▲ The Sport of Kings reigns supreme. Race meets are held year-round on superb grass courses. At the Curragh course in County Kildare, these thoroughbreds speed to the finish line in the two-day Budweiser Derby's opening event.
▶ What'll you bet? Sitting next to the jockeys' waiting room at the Curragh, this punter ponders his next wager.

◄ Tiny mayflowers blossom among the thirty-seven thousand hexagon-shaped basalt columns of the Giant's Causeway in County Antrim. Scientists say they are the result of massive volcanic eruptions some sixty million years ago, but local legend says it has more to do with a struggle between Fionn MacCumhaill (Finn MacCoul) and Scottish giant Finn Gall.
▲ Near the Giant's Causeway, rocky outcroppings such as these are strewn, as if from a giant's hand, all along the coast.

▲ More than three hundred national forests and parks, like Tollymore Forest Park near Newcastle in Northern Ireland, are scattered around Ireland. Some are small, undeveloped havens of nature trails, bird song, and tranquility, while others provide picnic sites and other visitor amenities. The country was stripped of some native trees thousands of years ago, but today there is an active reforestation program.

▶ East of the Giant's Causeway, flowers line a hiking trail.

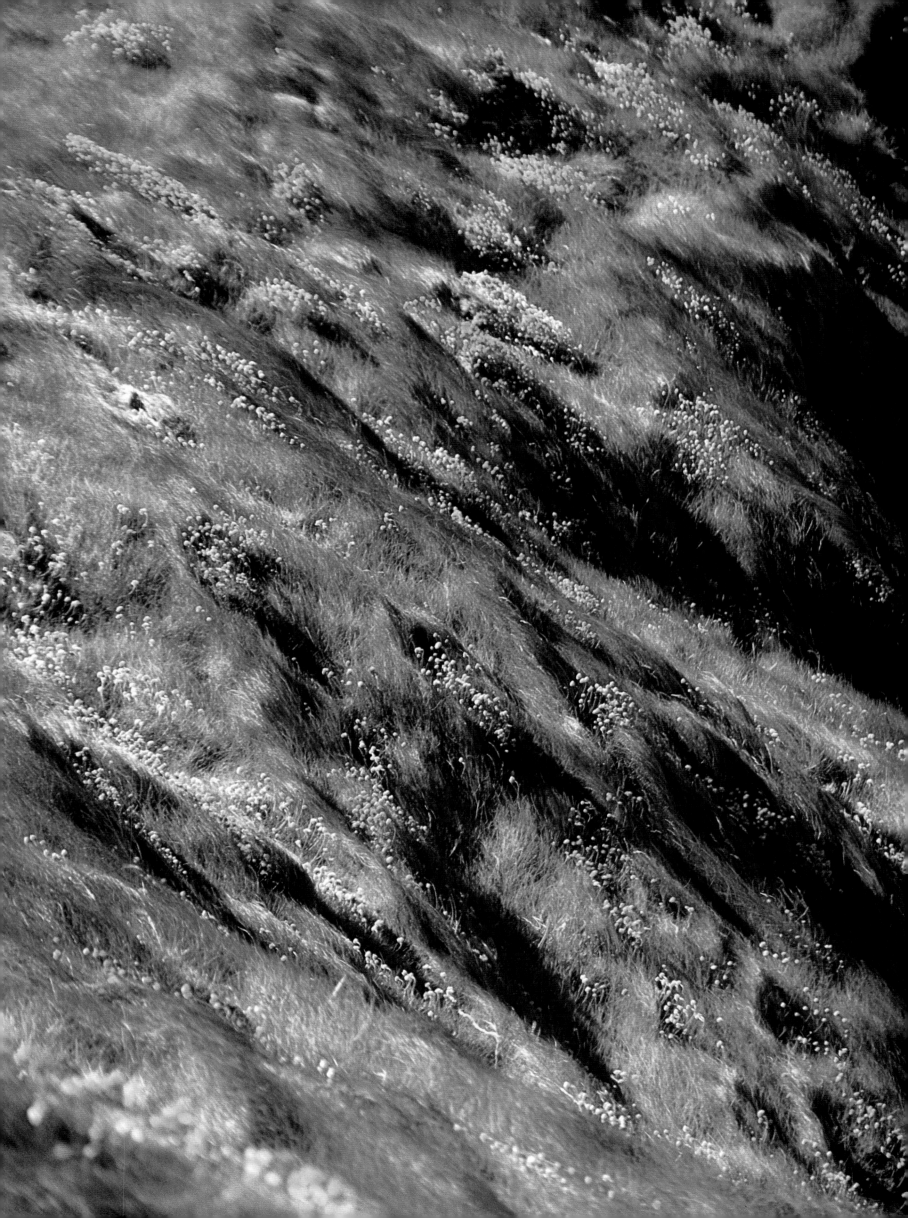

◄ Clouds are framed by an opening in the ruins of County Antrim's Dunluce Castle, whose cliff-top site has left it vulnerable to assault by the elements and by enemy armies.
▲ Ireland is a coarse, or freshwater, fishing paradise and lures thousands of sports lovers from around the world. In Northern Ireland, anglers cast their lines in rush-strewn rivers for bream, dace, pike, perch, and a number of hybrids.

▲ Still much revered in Belfast, Queen Victoria's likeness reigns over the City Hall as a reminder of her 1846 visit.
► The flowers on Northern Ireland's Carrick-a-Rede Island are just one reward for the brave of heart who make the crossing on its famous Rope Bridge, which is strung across a twenty-five-yard chasm above seas too treacherous for boats.

◄ Wind whispers through the grass near Dunluce Castle in County Antrim, a brooding silhouette against the horizon.
▲ Red-brick commercial buildings, relics of the nineteenth-century Industrial Revolution, evoke a time when Belfast prospered through its industries of linen and shipbuilding.
► ► Sunset lends a violet glow to the harbor in County Down's Newcastle. Situated on Dundrum Bay, the popular seaside resort is backed by the great bulk of Slieve Donard.

▲ Bemused by the photographer's attention, two old friends pose with typical Irish aplomb in Belleek, on the Donegal border in County Fermanagh. Internationally famous for its lustrous china, the town is also an important angling center.
▶ Near Newcastle, in County Down, the colorful gardens in Tollymore Forest Park display massive clumps of blooms, a legacy of those early settlers from England who brought their love of gardening with them to the north of Ireland.

◄ Immortalized in verse and song, "the mountains of Mourne slope down to the sea" near the sandy beach at Murlough Park, just north of Newcastle in County Down. Even their two-thousand-foot-plus peaks seem dwarfed by the three-thousand-foot-high Slieve Donard, which looms high over all.
▲ Fertile pastures and golden gorse need no voice to speak of beauty in County Down's Silent Valley, near Newcastle.

▲ Once home to the Butler family, impressive thirteenth-century Kilkenny Castle dominates the medieval town of Kilkenny. Cromwell made a right mess of it in 1649, but its Long Gallery today is a reflection of the gracious living that was experienced within its walls from its restoration in 1660 up to 1967 when the castle became public property.
▶ Kegs at Smithwick's Brewery in Kilkenny are used to store the lager known as "Smitty's" in Irish and continental pubs.

◄ At evening vespers in the vaulted sanctuary of Mount
Melleray monastery near Cappoquin in County Waterford,
Cistercian monks keep alive the traditions of their founders,
who were banished from France more than a century ago.
They transformed a bare mountainside into fertile fields.
▲ Sir Walter Raleigh, who introduced both tobacco and the
potato to Ireland, and *Moby Dick,* which was filmed here, left
their imprint on the fishing town of Youghal in County Cork.

▲ A master cutter carefully incises a classic pattern into a piece of Waterford Crystal. A unique blend of ingredients, fastidious mixing of raw materials, and skilled blowing produces Waterford's brilliance. So exacting are the standards that only two-thirds of the pieces make it to the cutters. The plant survived closure for a full century, from 1851 to 1951; today, some ninety thousand finished pieces leave Waterford every week, 60 percent of which go to the United States.

▲ Cape Clear Island off the West Cork coast holds one of Europe's few windmill-driven electricity generators, along with a small bird sanctuary, where hundreds of species are tracked in seasonal migrations. Ferry service from Baltimore on the mainland brings visitors to the island, whose Folk Museum relates the history of its Irish-speaking natives and their lifestyle, which is as rugged as the landscape.

▲ The 1739 Georgian mansion, Bantry Bay House, remains
the residence of descendants of its builder, Lord Bantry. Art
and antique collections are displayed, and its French Armada
Interpretive Centre describes the 1796 French attempt to
aid the Irish forces in their fight against British occupation.
▶ Much of the mystic Celtic past of this young Irish dancer
is preserved in the ancient designs of her costume, the music
to which she dances, and the intricate steps of her dance.

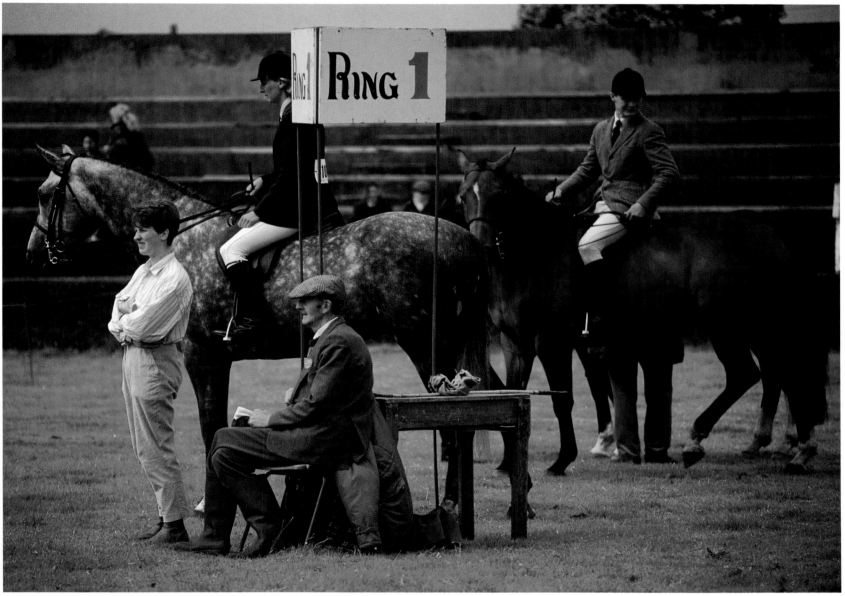

◄ A farmer leads his prize bull to the ring at the Skibbereen Agricultural Show in County Cork in southwest Ireland.
▲ ▲ Every animal must look its shining best before facing judges at the all-important annual Skibbereen competition.
▲ Fine horses and riders wait to compete in jumping meets.
► ► As much part of rural life as animals and fields, the Irish jig is on every Agricultural Show's list of events, and feet just finished with its joyous steps await the judges' decision.

▲ ▲ Sheep farmers huddle over the holding pen to assess
the chances of their entry's winning in the competition ring.
▲ In summer, Irish prayers for sunny weather ascend sky-
ward from those who race to beat the rain in "saving the hay."
▶ In County Cork, this lovely view of a small tower and its
lush surroundings is a pretty reward for those hardy enough
to make the 120-step climb to the summit of Blarney Castle.

◄ In a day, weather systems over Ireland can bring bright sun, dull clouds, and lashing rain. A ghostly mist may also add a special dimension to an enchanting landscape alive with relics of a past stretching back into the very mists of time.
▲ The waters along Cape Clear Island make the sea both friend and foe to its hardy residents, whose lives depend on highly developed skills in navigating its rocky shores.

▲ While many of the residents of Kinsale look seaward in pursuit of both commercial and pleasure boating, the surrounding fertile farmlands provide opportunity for a prosperous livelihood to an equal number of West Cork natives.
▶ Even though most Cape Clear Islanders are boat owners, they depend most heavily for travel to the mainland on the regularly scheduled ferry to Baltimore. This service is also vital for bringing in commodities that must be imported.

◄ Most of the shellfish that grace the tables of Ireland come from waters off the western seaboard. On the north coast of County Kerry's Iveragh Peninsula, just off the main Ring of Kerry route, lobster pots are an essential part of the local fishermen's trade in the little village of Portmagee.
▲ Unique to Ireland's west coast, the traditional *currach*, seen here in Portmagee, County Kerry, is a light skiff of tarred canvas, ideally suited to navigate hazardous waters.

▲ Tied up at the pier of County Kerry's Knightstown, the interior of this small fishing skiff provides temporary storage for the tools of its skipper's trade. The frail appearance of these boats is deceptive; they are well prepared for dangerous excursions several miles out to sea, aided by the skilled seamanship of fishermen who follow centures-old seafaring traditions to bring boat, crew, and catch safely back to port.

▲ The world-famous Lakes of Killarney are much loved. In the words of a jovial horse-and-trap driver, "Sure, 'tis a grand sight, one of God's blessings." Soft sunlight illuminates the shimmering water, rush-filled shoreline, and mountain background of one of the three lakes in all its fall glory. The sight lends credibility to legends that have grown up around the lakes based, it is said, on equal parts of truth and myth.

▲ From the beginning, dairy products have been important to Ireland's economy. In the past, farmers delivering large cans of milk to the local creamery by donkey and flatbed cart were a familiar sight on Irish roads. With the advent of the giant steel milk truck, a more common sight, even in such isolated locations as the Dingle Peninsula, is that of farmers passing the time of day while waiting for the truck to arrive.

▲ The glow of sunrise is reflected in the placid surface of one of the Lakes of Killarney, which hold as much appeal for their recreational possibilities as for their beauty. Swimming is permitted in all three lakes, and all are well stocked with fish. Anglers pay no charge to fish for brown trout, but the much-sought-after salmon must not be hooked without a license.

▲ The shores of Lakes of Killarney invite leisurely walks.
► The Atlantic surf beats against the jutting cliffs at Slea Head, the most westerly point in Europe, on the Dingle Peninsula in County Kerry. Next landfall, North America.
► ► A rainy night in small towns like Cahirciveen, in County Kerry, is excuse enough to send locals and visitors into a cozy pub for the evening, leaving streets deceptively deserted.

◄ Tools of the fishing trade at County Kerry's Portmagee are a mute witness to the village's close ties to the sea.
▲ "Sure, isn't it a lovely soft day," is the refrain of drivers, or "jarveys." Bundled up and soothed by the jarvey's repertoire of tall tales, passengers on the "jaunting car" en route to Muckross House in Killarney are likely in full agreement.

▲ Even though much of Ireland remains green year-round, autumn brings a splash of bright color across the landscape.
▶ The magnificent four-mile-long defile that is the Gap of Dunloe, just outside Killarney, bears evidence of considerable glacial action. Massive rocks rise on either side of the deep valley, and visitors are entranced by the celebrated echoes, which reverberate eerily between its rocky walls.

◄ Visitors who go around Lough Leane may choose to travel
by jaunting car, horse, or boat as they near the Gap of Dunloe.
▲ ▲ The Iron Age fortified strategic points on the Ring of
Kerry like Staigue Fort, with its mortar-free stone walls.
▲ Its worn oars attest to this Portmagee boat's long service.

▲ ▲ Thatched roofs, an integral part of Ireland's charm, make good use of the abundant supply of reeds, such as these reflected in the waters of Kilgory Lough in County Clare.
▲ Poulabrone Dolmen in County Clare's Burren is only one example of Ireland's megalithic monuments. Many dolmens were probably once covered with clay mounds or rock cairns.
▶ Haze lends a ghostly air to County Clare's Cliffs of Moher.

◄ The sheer, seven-hundred-foot drop of the Cliffs of Moher frames spectacular sea views, but the cliff edges are no place for the faint-hearted. Legend claims that in days of old many an unsuspecting traveler and/or enemy was lured too close to a deadly precipice and dispatched to a watery grave.
▲ Low walls constructed of stone slabs from the Cliffs of Moher prevent grazing cattle from straying over the edge.

▲ Dromoland Castle in County Clare is alive with tales of
colorful occupants, including Red Mary, who is said to have
married an English officer in order to hold onto her lands, then
assisted in his early death. Now a posh luxury hotel, its
medieval walled garden was the setting for many intrigues.
▶ The ruins of Quin Abbey in County Clare are relics of
a fifteenth-century monastery, which was constructed by
the MacNamaras on the site of a thirteenth-century castle.

◄ With nearly two hundred courses, many of them champion-ship class, Ireland attracts golfers like a magnet. Lahinch is regarded as one of the best and most difficult in Europe.
▲ Spectacular light shows, both above and below, are a frequent feature of sunset at County Clare's Kilgory Lough.
►► Against the night sky, the illuminated splendor of the Rock of Cashel is seen for miles across the surrounding plain.

▲ Modern-day Irish carry on traditions that date back to pre-Christian days as they celebrate, exalt, damn, lament, and mourn the circumstances of their lives in music and song. Musicians from around the world gather in O'Connor's Pub in County Clare's village of Doolin for spontaneous sessions.
▶ From childhood, the Irish intersperse playful romps on sandy beaches at resorts like Lahinch with an equally joyous search for crabs and other shellfish lurking under rocks.

◄ Driving on Ireland's small, wandering roads can be an adventure, with signposts written in both Irish and English and mileages shown in kilometers or miles. Add an occasional signpost that has been mysteriously turned around, and the chance of getting lost at least once is a virtual certainty.
▲ Played nowhere else, hurling draws crowds for championship matches such as this, where Tipperary defeated Cork.

▲ Well-groomed grounds like those of this extensive estate in eastern County Clare are in sharp contrast with the many small, rather shaggy farmlands throughout Ireland. Both reflect centuries of occupation and an imposed class system.
▶ Tidy, freshly whitewashed cottages, often brightened by colorful blooms, are a distinctive feature of the landscape of Ireland and underscore the deep love of house and home felt by most of the Irish, who highly value home ownership.

ACKNOWLEDGEMENTS

I would like to express my sincere appreciation to the IRISH TOURIST BOARD, both in Dublin and New York. Their assistance and guidance on the book provided entry into an intimate Ireland filled with special people and striking locales.

As well, I want to extend grateful thanks to DAN DOOLEY RENT A CAR who provided most of my transportation. With locations in several Irish cities and towns, they were a pleasure to deal with.

Finally, I would like to say a particular thank you to the many people who helped along the way – the landladies at our rental homes who introduced our kids to the neighbor children; the gas station attendants who knew a lovely little spot just down the road; the tolerant farmers and horse racers and fishermen who allowed me to buzz about them as they worked; and to all the others whose kindness and interest made this such a wonderful and memorable project.

TIM THOMPSON